Watch it Grow

An Apple's Life

Nancy Dickmann

www.raintreepublishers.co.uk
Visit our website to find out
more information about
Raintree books.

To order:

☎ Phone 0845 6044371

🖨 Fax +44 (0) 1865 312263

✉ Email myorders@raintreepublishers.co.uk

Customers from outside the UK please telephone +44 1865 312262

Raintree is an imprint of Capstone Global Library Limited,
a company incorporated in England and Wales having its
registered office at 7 Pilgrim Street, London, EC4V 6LB
– Registered company number: 6695582

Text © Capstone Global Library Limited 2010
First published in hardback in 2010
The moral rights of the proprietor have been asserted.

Edited by Nancy Dickmann, Rebecca Rissman, and Catherine Veitch
Designed by Joanna Hinton-Malivoire
Picture research by Mica Brancic
Production by Victoria Fitzgerald
Originated by Capstone Global Library Ltd
Printed and bound in China by South China Printing
Company Ltd

ISBN 978 0 431 19539 1
14 13 12 11 10
10 9 8 7 6 5 4 3 2 1

British Library Cataloguing in Publication Data
Dickmann, Nancy.
Apple. -- (Watch it grow)
583.7'3-dc22

Acknowledgements
We would would like to thank the following for permission to reproduce
photographs: Alamy pp. **9** (© Mode Images Limited), **10** (© Nigel Cattlin),
22 right (© Nigel Cattlin), **23 middle** (© Mode Images Limited), **23
bottom** (© Nigel Cattlin); FLPA p. **8** (© Nigel Cattlin); iStockphoto pp. **4**
(© Eric Michaud), **5** (© gaffera), **7** (© lillisphotography), **12** (© Ints
Tomsons), **15** (© Dmitry Ckalev), **17** (© Hayri Er), **19** (© Patty Colabuono),
20 (© Dianne Maire), **22 top** (© Dianne Maire), **22 bottom** (© Hayri
Er), **22 left** (© gaffera); Photolibrary pp. **13** (imagebroker.net/© Herbert
Kehrer), **14** (Garden Picture Library/© Mark Bolton), **18** (Animals
Animals/© Donald Specker), **21** (Garden Picture Library/© Mark Bolton);
Shutterstock pp. **6** (© Valery Potapova), **11** (© constant), **16** (© Gorilla),
23 top (© Gorilla).

Front cover photograph (main) of apples on a branch reproduced with
permission of iStockphoto (© Viorika Prikhodko). Front cover photograph
(inset) of a close-up of a green apple pip reproduced with permission of
iStockphoto (© Dianne Maire). Back cover photograph of apple blossom
reproduced with permission of iStockphoto (© Dmitry Ckalev).

The publisher would like to thank Nancy Harris for her assistance in the
preparation of this book.

Every effort has been made to contact copyright holders of material
reproduced in this book. Any omissions will be rectified in subsequent

Contents

Life cycles

All living things have a life cycle.

An apple has a life cycle.

seed

Inside an apple there are seeds.
The seeds will grow into a new
apple tree.

The new apple tree will grow apples.
Later it will die.

Seeds and shoots

An apple seed grows in the ground.

roots

Roots grow down from the seed into the ground.

shoot

A shoot grows up from the seed.

leaves

Leaves grow from the shoot.

Becoming a tree

The young tree needs water and sunlight to grow.

The young tree grows bigger.

The tree grows new leaves in
the spring.

flower

The tree grows flowers in the spring.

Making apples

pollen

A bee comes to feed on a flower.
The bee has pollen on it.

The pollen helps make new apple
seeds grow on the tree.

Then an apple starts to grow.

When the apples have grown some
fall from the tree.

seed

The apple has seeds inside it.

The life cycle starts again.

Life cycle of an apple tree

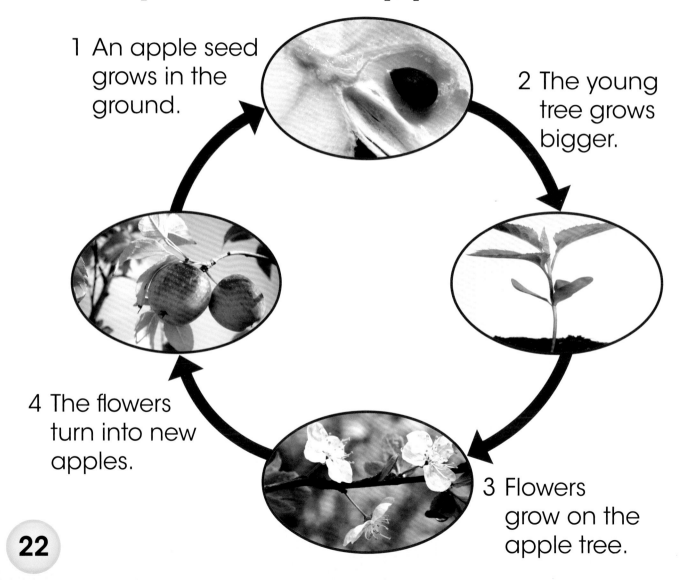

1 An apple seed grows in the ground.

2 The young tree grows bigger.

3 Flowers grow on the apple tree.

4 The flowers turn into new apples.

22

Picture glossary

pollen yellow powder inside
a flower

root part of a plant that grows
underground. Roots take up water
for the plant to use.

shoot small green stem that grows
from a seed

Index

Notes to parents and teachers

Before reading

Show the children an apple and ask them if they know how apples grow. Ask them what will be inside if you cut the apple open. Slice open the apple and look at the seeds together. What else do they know that grows from seeds?

After reading

• Talk to the children about the Jewish New Year, Rosh Hashanah. Explain how it is a tradition for Jewish people to eat apples dipped in honey during this festival so that they will have a sweet new year. Let the children dip a slice of apple each into some honey so they can try this.

• Tell the children the story of Johnny Appleseed and how he planted apple orchards in the United States. Talk about how important it is to plant new trees. Maybe you could plant an apple tree together in the school grounds.